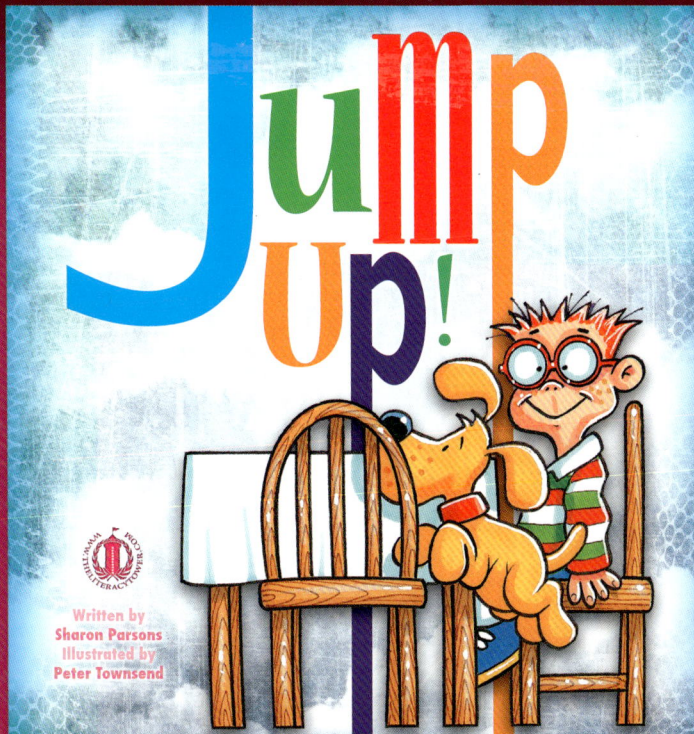

JuMp Up!

Written by
Sharon Parsons
Illustrated by
Peter Townsend

a dog

a boy

"In this story,
a dog does
what it is told.
But at the end,
the dog tells
a cat what to do!"

Grusilda xxx

a mum and dad

"Jump up!" said the boy.

The dog jumped up.

"Get down!" said Mum.

The dog got down.

"Jump in!" said Dad.

The dog jumped in.

"Jump out!" said the dog.

The cat jumped out!